TABLE OF CONTENTS

SEEING THROUGH THE CONFLICT: MILITARY-MEDIA RELATIONS

As our country moves closer to a forced regime change in Iraq, the Department of Defense should anticipate that the media will cover this next conflict with as much intensity as they displayed during the Gulf War. During the Gulf War, more than 1600 journalists converged on the Joint Information Bureaus in Dhahran and Riyadh, Saudi Arabia.[1] We can expect no less if and when we go to war with Iraq. The question is, however, will the military be up to the task of supporting this massive convergence?

Tensions between the media have been present in our society since the Revolutionary War, but may have reached its peak of hostility during the Vietnam War. By the end of this conflict, a greater distrust and suspicion developed between the military and the media. Many in the military claimed that the news media, with its graphic portrayal of the war's brutality, lost the war for America.   Many in the media counter this position by saying it was the military that, by providing falsehoods and propaganda, lost America's confidence in prosecuting the war any further. Although 30 years have gone by since the end of America's involvement in the war in Vietnam, some believe this conflict still is unresolved.

As we enter the 21st century, the world no longer relies on information but on real-time information. Today's media, with its global reach and real-time capability due to satellite technology, dominates this new information age.   World leaders are now able to turn to the media for instant access to national and international incidents as they unfold, and they can do so 24-hours per day. This instant access by the media to world events now circumvents well-established intelligence activities and as a result, real-time media has become a part of their decision-making.

The former President Bush once told world leaders that he learned more from CNN than he did from the CIA.[2] In addition, many people may recall seeing pictures of the current President Bush watching TV at a Florida elementary school on September 11, 2001, as the World Trade Center burned and eventually collapsed.

At the time of this writing, war is already being fought between the U.S. and Iraq, but it is a war with information. The U.S. has leveraged its use of images of troops deploying while the Iraqis are allowing unprecedented numbers of international media into its country, both sides hoping to shape national and international public perceptions and thus, public opinion.

The stakes are high in this information war. What happens now at the tactical level can be leveraged by an adversary to have strategic importance and consequence. It is therefore, critically important that the U.S. military be prepared to fight what former Air Force Chief of Staff

General Ronald R. Fogleman once said is now the fifth dimension of warfare…information operations.[3]

The focus of this paper is to address only one of the key enablers to information operations—military public affairs. Former Chief of Army Public Affairs, Major General Charles W. McClain Jr., stated in an article titled "Public Affairs in America's 21st Century Army," that information would be a center of gravity on future battlefields.[4] He added, "On the battlefield, it [public affairs] is as essential an element of mission success, as important a combat multiplier, and as critical a component of building and sustaining combat power as any of the Battlefield Operating Systems, especially when the global media is a significant element of battle space.[5]

Numerous articles, books, and even a scattering of academic research have been written during the last 10 years that conclude that there remains much acrimony to the military-media relations debate. Additionally, recent military after action reviews, that when dissected and compared with what journalists have said about the military-media relationship, produce consistent common lessons learned as to why a perceived conflict may remain between the media and the military.

Key to understanding the current debate is to review and appreciate what others have said about military-media relationships and historical events, which have guided military and media relations up to this point. After all, war correspondents for more than 200 years have often shared many of the same challenges that correspondents do today, such as a perceived lack of access, lack of support, and censorship by the military.

PREVIOUS STUDIES

Prior to the 1991 Gulf War, scholarly research regarding military public affairs is rather sparse. This is not to say that articles and books have not been written that address military public affairs operations, but these works are predominately anecdotal in context and are mainly written by journalists. Nevertheless, a review of a selection of recent research and literature may provide some useful insight into military public affairs successes, failures, or challenges.

In 1996, Pascale Combelles-Siegel conducted a study titled The Troubled Path to the Pentagon's Rules on Media Access to the Battlefield: Grenada to Today. In this study, Combelles-Siegel investigated the perceived military-media conflict and stated that this relationship "exploded like a bomb" during Operation Urgent Fury in Grenada.[6] It is no secret that upon the end of the U.S. involvement in Vietnam, that many in the military harbored ill feelings toward the media. As a result, this Vietnam "baggage" carried by the media may have assured their exclusion from military operations in Grenada for the first three days.

2

Combelles-Siegel highlights that this exclusion not only outraged the media, but also some in the Department of Defense. Michael Burch, then Assistant Secretary of Defense for Public Affairs, said, "A combination of mistrust, poor planning, and poor execution on the part of the commander who did not realize that it would have helped the image of the operation and helped gather international support for the operation." Additionally, Navy Captain Robert Sims, spokesperson for the National Security Council, said, "Because the press was excluded, the operation received unfavorable reporting, even though it was a staunch success.[7]

Combelles-Siegel followed the military public affairs efforts from Grenada through the Gulf War and concluded on a positive note regarding the future of the military-media relationship because of 10 years of military-media compromises. Nevertheless, as hopeful as she was for a better relationship, she believed that the military still had serious shortfalls in its long-term plan to accommodate the media.[8]

Her main concern was that the large numbers of media that cover future conflicts would overwhelm the military. She recommended that the military find some way to limit the numbers of media who cover U.S. military operations in order to provide adequate logistical support to the media. This recommendation, however, may work well in a conflict such as Grenada, where the area of operations was on an island, but it may not be realistic to believe that the U.S. military can control access to a conflict that takes place on a continent. For example, unless the U.S. could seal all the borders with Iraq it is not likely the U.S. could control the flow, if not the flood, of media into Iraq if the U.S. liberates that country.

In the book titled Distorting Defense, Stephen P. Aubin provides an interesting insight to the media's coverage of defense issues. Although Aubin's book does not specifically address the military-media relationship his research does, however, look at how the media has covered defense-related issues.

Aubin conducted a content analysis, in essence a sampling, of the major networks (ABC, NBC, and CBS) evening broadcasts of defense-related issues during the Reagan, Bush, and Clinton Administrations. He claimed that since the colonial times in America, the nation and the nation's media have been suspicious, if not openly hostile, toward defense-related issues. The American people, according to Aubin, have for more than 200 years preferred less expensive routes toward the nation's security.[9]

Additionally, the content analysis Aubin conducted found that nearly 32 percent of the evening news coverage of defense issues was problematic.[10] Aubin defined "problematic coverage as: general lack of balance or context; lack of context as a result of brevity; lack of knowledge on the par of the correspondent; overemphasis on drama or bad news at the expense of substance and context; loaded labeling or advocacy; and bad news judgment.

The picture that Aubin paints in his historical review is that it has been and may always be a hard sell for the military to promote to the American people the importance of new weapons systems, an increase in defense spending, or the deployment of U.S. troops into conflict. If one now couples that thought with what Aubin found in his content analysis regarding problematic news coverage of defense issues, the U.S. military's public affairs has some very big hurdles to overcome in telling the military story. The implication for the military may be that the American people, and especially the media, will continue to be very critical of its operations. The military must understand that what they perceive as good news stories may not be perceived as good news by the American people. And, that bad news stories may be perceived as being worse than they actually are due to the more than 200 years of a predisposition by the media and by the American people.

In 2001, LTC Joseph G. Curtin, U.S. Army, conducted a Strategy Research Project titled <u>Strategic Leaders: It's Time to Meet the Press</u>. His research examined the media environment, challenges, and prospects for improving strategic leader relations with the press.[11]

After reviewing historical perspectives between the media and the military, Curtin stated, "Despite the lessons learned from one military operation to the next since Vietnam, the military-media relationship continues to sour."[12] I, however, do not necessarily agree with Curtin's assessment that the military-media relationship has not improved through the years. One need only watch the weekly Pentagon Press briefings or watch today's reporting of troops deploying to Iraq to see that the military-media relationship has come a long way in its professionalism since the dark days of the Vietnam War.

Despite Curtin's dour opinion of the current military-media relationship, he does believe that there is hope to improving this relationship, but only if strategic leaders take action. He recommended that strategic leaders consider:

- That the Defense Information School at Fort Meade, Maryland, designs and implements a short-course in media relations for senior leaders.
- That strategic leaders establish professional relationships with members of the press.
- That the Defense Department (DoD) reestablishes a public affairs office in Chicago.
Evidently DoD had earlier closed down this office as part of the military's downsizing, but has kept public affairs offices open in Los Angeles and New York. Curtain saw a gap in the military's ability to reach the major media markets in the mid-West region.

- -As senior leaders mentor subordinates, they should include media relations as part of that mentorship. [13]

THE JOURNALISTS

"We saw an Army public affairs system fashioned as a dead-end job career for officers and staffed with a sprinkling of incompetents put there by media-wary generals, some of whom still blame the media for losing the Vietnam War."

--John J. Fialka, Wall Street Journal

The U.S. media arrived home after their stint in the Gulf War only to find that they had something in common with the Iraqi military—both had been soundly defeated by the U.S. military. President George Bush said prior to Gulf War hostilities that "this conflict would not be like Vietnam."[14] For some in the media, President Bush was right. Unlike the war in Vietnam where the media roamed freely over the battlefield, the Gulf War media found themselves subjected to a military public affairs system that restricted their access to the troops.[15]

"On a scale unprecedented in our history, politics and propaganda became criteria in news coverage of the U.S. at war. Sensitivities governed access decisions, with the military acting as news assignment editors," said 17 leaders of the U.S. media in a protest letter to Secretary of Defense Richard Cheney in July 1991.[16] These leaders condemned the military public affairs system and described the Gulf War as "the most under-covered major conflict in modern American history.[17]

Reporters acknowledge that restrictions are necessary in wartime, but many allege the Pentagon went beyond legitimate security concerns during the Gulf War and attempted to present the American public a sanitized version of war.[18]

John J. Fialka's book titled Hotel Warriors is also an excellent starting point for discussion when reviewing what the media have recently said about working with the military. Fialka, then a reporter for the Wall Street Journal, had covered defense-related issues since the 1970s. In the Gulf War, Fialka was one of the print media pool coordinators who had the awesome responsibility for assigning fellow print reporters to the pool.

Fialka painted a bleak picture of military support, via the military public affairs officers, to the media during the Gulf War. The military's support, according to Fialka, bordered on near collapse. Everything from a military public affairs operation that sorely lacked required resources to media wary generals contributed to what Fialka said "helped bury one of the most positive Army stories since World War II."[19]

In an article titled "Pentagon Hardball," David Lamb, a national correspondent for the Los Angeles Times during the Gulf War, also echoed Fialka's comments. Lamb reported that the military was not able to handle the shear volumes of media who were arriving at a rate of 50 per day.[20] He said that at one point the Joint Information Bureau (JIB) had a backlog of 1,300 requests by reporters to visit units. Because of this poor support, Lamb said that most correspondents could not get out to cover the military units and thus, were relegated to rewriting the Gulf War.[21]

The other area that Lamb highlighted is the perceived non-support from the senior military leadership. For example, he stated that the 24th Infantry Division entered combat without one correspondent and that the unit "might as well not have existed" to Americans back home.[22] "Younger brigade and battalion commanders—most of all, their troops—welcomed us with enthusiasm and looked on us as their link to home, many of the generals viewed us as some alien force that could be detrimental to morale and mission."[23]

HISTORICAL PERSPECTIVES

REVOLUTIONARY WAR: IN THE BEGINNING...

> "They that give up essential liberty to obtain a little temporary safety deserve neither liberty or safety."
>
> —Benjamin Franklin

Colonial newspapers during the Revolutionary period may not have been well written, but they were well read. Newspapers went into about 40,000 homes, but unlike today, every word was read by a public that was thirsting for information about the conflict. Newspapers of the period also enjoyed a long shelf life as they were passed from one household to another, rarely being discarded.[24] In essence, the local paper had become the community bulletin board.

Generals fighting for and against independence quickly realized the power of the press. General George Washington, for example, used the press not only to influence public opinion and thus, public support, but also to maintain the fighting spirit of his forces.[25] Realizing the importance of maintaining public support, both Tory and the colonialist used the press extensively for self-serving reasons during America's fight for independence. Both sides, either by force or by persuasion, used the press that was sympathetic to their cause as a tool of propaganda.

Sitting on the fence, so to speak, was not an option for the editors. Printers took unprecedented risk of not only business failure, but also of death to support their cause. Because of this partiality by the editors, Tory and colonial military forces often literally chased many printers out of business. Additionally, if the editors survived the Tory and colonial governments then they still had to deal with public opinion. The public, with strong divided sympathies between the Tory and colonial cause, often turned to mob action as a form of censorship of a printer who did not support their cause. As a result, most newspaper printers at the beginning of the conflict were forced out of business by the end of the Revolutionary War.[26]

Given the often biased and at times libelous reporting, it is interesting to note that the framers of the Constitution and the Bill of Rights would still allow journalists in the First Amendment the tremendous freedom of an unrestricted press, fully understanding how the press was used and could be used in the future.

Therefore, to answer the question posed by some in today's military of who gave the press freedom to cover and report to the American public, they earned their right in one of the most trying times in American history. In no small way, the colonial press played a very large part in saving the colonies from British oppression. As a result, the American press was rewarded for its support during the Revolution when Congressional delegates to the Constitutional Convention ratified the First Amendment in 1791.

CIVIL WAR: THE NOT SO CIVIL PRESS...

> "Come with a sword or musket in your hand, prepared to share with us our fate in sunshine and storm...and I will welcome you as a brother and associate; but come as you now do, expecting me to ally the reputation and honor of my country and my fellow soldiers with you, as a representative of the press, which you yourself say make so slight a difference between the truth and falsehood, and my answer is, NEVER."

> —General Sherman to the NY Herald

By the time of the South's shelling of Fort Sumpter in April 1861, the news media went through a revolution in media technology and may have been better prepared to cover the war than the military was in executing the war. In the 30 or so years leading up to the American Civil War, the press underwent a revolution in technology and techniques in reporting. Not only did newspapers become affordable to the masses with the penny press, but publishers also became able to print thousands of newspapers per day because of dramatic advances in printing press technology. Additionally, the media led the way leveraging technology, via 50,000 miles of telegraph lines and railroads. Correspondents at the front could now observe a battle and have their story received by their newspaper headquarters within hours.[27]

At the beginning of the war, the military had not fully leveraged technology as well as the media. The military, for the most part, relied on trains that could travel at two miles a minute, or carrier pigeons that could reach speeds of 35 miles per hour. Meanwhile, the media used the telegraph that could transmit a story at the speed of light--186,000 miles per second.[28]

Despite this revolution in technology, there appeared to be no revolution in the media's professionalism. Newspaper editors found that news of battles could raise circulation five-fold.[29] War reporters often found that "immediacy" of a story was more important than accuracy or even operational security. Both Northern and Southern generals found the media an annoyance that they attempted to control. In 1863, Northern General Joseph Hooker tried to improve the responsibility of reporting by mandating that reporters traveling with him had to use a byline that gave the reporter's name in the article, a practiced still used by today's media.[30]

Some generals, such as William Tecumseh Sherman, took a harsher way of dealing with the press by banishing them from his camps. As a result, however, General Sherman's successful operation from Atlanta to the coast went relatively unreported.[31] And, there were some in the military who, for reasons of maintaining public morale, lied to the press. Edwin Stanton, President Lincoln's secretary of war, altered casualty figures so that the numbers looked much better than reality.[32]

By the end of the war, the rise of professional war correspondents also brought about the rise to the military-media conflict and the stage was now set for all future conflicts. The military saw the impact that the media could have on public opinion as well as on the morale of their troops. The military also realized that they began the war unprepared for the media. There were no uniform press guidelines or trained military personnel to deal with the press. Nor, did the military leverage technology as well as the media. The military's lesson was that no matter what restraints that they might impose on the media, media will always find a way to report the war.

"The last war, during the years of 1915, 1916, 1917 was the most colossal, murderous, mismanaged butchery that has ever taken place on earth. Any writer who said otherwise lied. So the writers either wrote propaganda, shut up, or fought."

—Ernest Hemingway

In the 70 years prior to WWI, more than 37 million immigrants entered the United States.[33] Unsure of the allegiance of these immigrants, the U.S. government in 1917, established new censorship guidelines with the Espionage Act. To strengthen that act, an amendment called the Trading with the Enemy Sedition Act was added in 1918.[34] These acts essentially made it illegal to make opinions or statements that may be disloyal to the government or to the military. A reporter who became in violation of these acts faced up to 20 years in prison.[35]

In addition to these acts, President Woodrow Wilson issued executive orders giving power to the U.S. military to control the media. General John J. Pershing, with newly given authority, followed the administration's censorship lead by publishing General Order Number 36 that required American newsmen be accredited. This accreditation meant a lengthy process that included a personal appearance before the Secretary of War, an oath to write the truth, and by submitting a $10,000 bond to ensure their proper conduct in the field.[36]

The U.S. government also used formal propaganda to sway public opinion. In 1917, President Wilson established the Committee on Public Information, known as the Creel Commission because of its chairman, George Creel. Creel, a former journalist, built an anti-German propaganda machine that touched Americans wherever they received information. From newspapers to movie theaters, Creel mounted a propaganda campaign that was unprecedented in American history.[37]

For the first time in American history, the government controlled the pictures as well as shaped the words of journalists. Some may call it a sense of patriotism that ensured journalists wrote about the war in a way that raised the morale of the American people, while others may be more cynical and say that reporters conformed to press censorship in order to gain access to the troops. Regardless the reason, the Wilson Administration left no doubt in anyone's mind that, unlike during the Civil War, the U.S. government was prepared to handle the press. But, at what cost? One may only wonder how many stories of heroism, success, and failure on the battlefield will never be known because of stringent press restrictions. Phillip Knightly, in The

First Casualty, recounts many untold stories due to military censorship in WWI. According to Knightly, no one will ever know the true extent of lives lost because journalists were restricted from reporting the war.[38]

Nevertheless, two important philosophical points came out of WWI military-media relations. First, the military can impose censorship, censorship that will be understood and accepted by the American public to ensure the nation's defense. Secondly, in times of war there is tremendous value of using propaganda as a tool to raise the nation's morale as well as to degrade the morale of its adversary.[39]

WWII: PATRIOTIC CENSORSHIP

> "As long as all copy was submitted to censors before transmission, people in the field, from generals down, felt free to discuss top secret material with reporters."
>
> —Drew Middleton of the New York Times

The attack on Pearl Harbor by the Japanese on December 7, 1941, sparked a fear in all Americans that their way of life would never be the same again. With a common cause and determination, Americans were united in a sense of patriotism not felt since WWI and far be it for the American media to stifle that sense of patriotism. Joseph J. Matthews, in his book titled Reporting the Wars, described this self-imposed attitude of the American media as "necessary in order to eliminate hindrances to the conduct of war."[40]

The American novelist John Steinbeck added, "Certain people could not be criticized or even questioned. The foolish reporter who broke the rules would not be printed at home and in addition would be put out of the theater by the command...Gradually it became a part of all of us that the truth about anything was automatically secret and that to trifle with it was to interfere...By this I don't mean that the correspondents were liars. They were not. It is in the things not mentioned that the untruth lies."[41]

The U.S. government and military quickly built upon lessons learned from WWI regarding censorship and propaganda. Roosevelt believed that censorship was a military function and that propaganda was a strategic weapon and so, he separated the two functions.[42] Within eleven days of the Japanese attack on Pearl Harbor, President Roosevelt created the U.S. Office of Censorship, but it would take until1942 before Roosevelt established the Office of War Information.[43]

An interesting aspect of Roosevelt's censorship plan called for the press and radio to abstain voluntarily from disseminating detailed information about such things as troop and vessel movements. There were no fines or prescribed jail time for non-compliance of the censorship rules. For the most part, American reporters were caught up in the patriotism fervor and complied with self-censorship. Where the system broke down, however, was with some of the senior military leadership. Although denial of access seemed to be the preferred method of military censorship, some leaders did censorship the old-fashioned way — by intimidation and coercion. For example, General Douglas MacArthur "routinely required correspondent's copy to go through multiple censorship reviews and pressured journalists to produce stories that burnished the image of troops and their supreme commander."[44] For fear of damaging troop morale and loosing even more support from back home, MacArthur quickly placed correspondents under Army control and imposed strict censorship.

What did come about the WWII military-media relationship, however, were the concepts of "pooling" and embedding media. The military used pooling because of the difficulty of supporting the large numbers of war correspondents. It has been estimated that more than 10,000 journalists covered WWII.[45] The media pools allowed for a representative from a like-type of media, print or broadcast, to follow a unit into action. That media representative then covered the actions of that unit and shared his or her media products with all reporters, regardless of affiliation. Although reporters did not like the pool system, it became a necessary evil in order to cover the war.

When one thinks of WWII embedded media, the image of Ernie Pyle immediately comes to mind. Pyle, with his humanizing of the soldiers' plight, won the hearts and minds of soldiers and the American public alike. He traveled with military units as they fought in North Africa and Europe, and was killed in the South Pacific by Japanese machinegun fire. His reporting style set the standard for the future of embedded media by showing that reporters and the military can work closely together and surprisingly, get along with each other.

But with the end of WWII, the apex of media-military cooperation may have ended, too. During the war, correspondents had become just as integral to America's fight as were the troops on the battlefield. Throughout the war, correspondents traveled with the troops, wore the same clothes as the troops, and suffered right along with the troops.[46] This level of mutual understanding and respect between the media and the military would be only a footnote in history books by the time of America's involvement in Vietnam.

VIETNAM: WHERE ARE THE ERNIE PYLE'S?

> "There is a tendency in the military to blame our problems with lack of (American) public support on the media. This is too easy an answer. The majority of the on-the-scene (Vietnam) reporting was factual—that is, the reporters honestly reported what they had seen, firsthand. Much of what they saw was horrible, for that is the nature of war. It was this horror, not the reporting, that so influenced the American people."
>
> —Col. (Ret.) Harry Summers

Some would think that after 30 years, the ghosts of the Vietnam military-media relationship would have been silenced by now. Nevertheless, the debate rages on in some circles in the military today just as loudly as it may have back in 1973. Today's U.S. Army War College students were too young to serve during Vietnam, but it has been interesting to observe that in many seminar discussions it seems that the ghosts of the Vietnam still live. In essence, several students often refer to today's media as being anti-military and use Vietnam-era analogies to support their positions. One seminar officer said that he even believes that all media should be under government control because they (media) cannot be trusted.[47]

When reviewing recent articles written by American journalists, such as in CBS.MarketWatch and the Columbia Journalism Review, references to the Vietnam media-military media relations are common.[48] It appears that the media still harbor ghosts, too, because when conflicts arise with the military some in the media reflect to Vietnam.

But, Vietnam was different as the U.S. military broke with previous war public affairs efforts by not imposing press censorship. According to William M. Hammond in his The Army and Public Affairs: Enduring Principles, "General William C. Westmoreland, in consultation with agencies in Washington, opted for a policy of voluntary guidelines for the press over censorship because he trusted the good will of the American correspondents reporting the war."[49]

It may have been this lack of military censorship that added to the conflict between the military and the media. The press roamed the battlefields in Vietnam with relatively no control by the U.S. military. Very similar to the Civil War press, the media of the '60s leveraged technology as Americans became glued to television for their daily news. This combination of a free press armed with television now brought the horrors of the war into the homes of America. As the war continued year after year, American's became more attuned to the sights and sounds of war and the evening news often told a different story than was being told by President Johnson's administration.[50] This disconnect between reality and the administration's Vietnam public relations strategy may have been the catalyst that caused Americans to turn pessimistic regarding our involvement in Vietnam.

In a 1984 Proceedings article written by Richard L. Upchurch, he said, "Vietnam in the early '70s was portrayed as a war of brutal death, vice a struggle for victory and democracy. Reporters collected all the stench, gore, and never-ending suffering of war on film and brought it into the living rooms of every American who had a television. Tally boards depicting the number killed or wounded for the week kept the public constantly reminded of just how badly the war was going."[51]

But it was more than just the typical American who turned to TV for information about the war--President Johnson had three televisions set up in the Oval Office so that he could watch all three major TV networks at the same time.[52] The affect that television news has on decision makers was now evident at the highest levels of U.S. leadership.

GRENADA & PANAMA: GHOSTS OF VIETNAM

> "...the decision was made by the commanders to whom we entrusted this dangerous mission to withhold from the press advance notification of the Grenada operation and to keep reporters and other noncombatants off...until the American citizens were safe."
>
> —Secretary of Defense Casper Weinberger

In the 10 years since the end of the U.S. involvement in Vietnam, the ghosts of Vietnam still haunted both the military and the media. The military whose image was still hurting from the televised war in Vietnam had done very little between conflicts to bridge the gulf between itself and the media. The media, meanwhile, still had a sense of distrust of the military to tell them the truth. And so, the stage was set in 1983 when U.S. forces were thrust into action in Grenada. The division between the media and the military may have been just as wide as it was 10 years earlier when the U.S. pulled its last combat troops out of Vietnam.[53]

For the first time in American history, the military excluded the media from reporting Americans in combat. The commander of the Grenada operation was Vice Admiral Joseph Metcalf, and he initially made no apologies for his decision to exclude the media for the first two days of the operation. Afterwards, however, he changed his mind arguing that the press ban was counterproductive because it resulted in depriving the American public a great story about its military.[54]

The media's uproar of being left behind prompted the Defense Department to commission retired Major General Winant Sidle to investigate the military-media relationship. The Sidle Panel agreed with the media that much work was needed by the military to ensure adequate coverage of future military operations. The Panel suggested that: public affairs planning should begin as soon as operational planning begins; the military should establish a media pool until such time as open coverage could be arranged; and the military should provide essential logistical equipment to assist reporters covering the operation.[55]

This new guidance went largely unimplemented in the military's first major test of these guidelines during the United States' invasion of Panama in 1989. The invasion went relatively uncovered because the military deployed once again without the media. Due to concerns with operational security, Secretary of Defense Richard Cheney decided not to deploy the media pool in a timely manner nor did he allow for the establishment of a media pool in Panama.[56]

Once again, the Pentagon commissioned another panel, this one led by Fred Hoffman, a former Associated Press reporter who had covered the Pentagon, to review military-media relations. Hoffman's lead findings were that the military did not place sufficient importance on planning for the media, and that the Deputy Assistant Secretary of Defense for Public Affairs should have monitored the development of military public affairs operations more closely.[57]

The next test of the military's attempt to accommodate the media came during the Gulf War, where it revealed that neither the Sidle nor the Hoffman recommendations had been wholly embraced by the military.

GULF WAR: CENSORSHIP OR POOR PLANNING?

> "One of the earliest casualties in America's desert war was the truth. The truth was wounded by an information directorate bent on controlling the words and images that flow from the battlefields and clogged the vital artery leading to America's brain."
>
> - Joseph Galloway, U.S. News and World Report

By the time the U.S. entered the Gulf War, lessons learned from the Sidle and Hoffman Commissions were forgotten or ignored by the military. The Pentagon made it quite clear that it would manage the war reporting by establishing completely new guidelines for media coverage.[58]

Until January 1991, the media had relatively free rein in Saudi Arabia to cover U.S. military operations with the only restrictions being the actual location of troops and material.[59]

14

Nevertheless, in January 1991, Pete Williams, Assistant Secretary of Defense for Public Affairs, developed new press guidelines that went into effect once the war broke out in the Gulf Region. The guidelines included the following restrictions:[60]

- All reporters in combat areas had to belong to officially designated media pools and had to be escorted by military public affairs officers.
- All stories on film filed by the pools would be subject to a "security review" by the accompanying public affairs officers.
- Information deemed by the Pentagon to be "unreleasable" for security reasons included the exact locations of U.S. military units, data on troop strength or the number of armaments, and the disclosures of downed U.S. planes or the sinking of U.S. ships.
- Written descriptions of, or broadcasts showing, severely wounded U.S. military personnel would be discouraged, but allowed.
- Impromptu interviews with U.S. military officers could be conducted only in public places and the interviews had to be "on record."
- Journalists considered physically unfit by U.S. commanders would be subject to medical evaluation from the front lines.

The Pentagon saw these rules as essential to ensure the safety of troops and the reporters. But, a well-respected journalist and former CBS News anchorman, Walter Cronkite, wrote in a February 1991, Newsweek article, "The U.S. military is trampling on the American people's right to know...but the fact that we don't know, the fact that the military apparently feels there is something to hide, can only lead eventually to a breakdown in home-front confidence and the very echoes from Vietnam that the Pentagon fears the most.[61]

Nevertheless, reporters' anger with the U.S. military may not be solely due to the Department of Defense guidelines or censorship. There are some in the media and military who believe the large numbers of the press simply overwhelmed an unprepared U.S. military public affairs effort.

According to U.S. News & World Report columnist David Gergen, the total number of media personnel in the Gulf exceeded 1,500 by the time the ground war began. All major networks (NBC, CBS, ABC, and CNN) sent their news anchors to the Gulf for on-the-spot reporting. "Experts were hired and budgets wrecked," Gergen wrote.[62] John Fialka of the Wall

Street Journal adds, "We were an indigestible lump being fed into a military press-handling system that was woefully short of resources and teetering on the verge of collapse."[63]

Pascale Combelles-Siegel states in her study of the media's access to the battlefield that Navy Captain Mike Sherman, who was the Joint Information Bureau [JIB] director in Dhahran, claimed that he not only was not resourced to run the JIB, but also that the U.S. Central Command was slow to direct units to cooperate with the JIB. "We were the bastard children of the operation," Sherman is quoted as saying.[64]

According to LTC Robert Perrich, an Army public affairs officer who participated in Desert Shield and Desert Storm, "The bottom line is that there was no command planning or priority directed to public affairs." As a result, only about 10 percent of the accredited reporters ever made it to the front lines.[65]

TODAY'S MILITARY PUBLIC AFFAIRS...SURELY WE ARE BETTER OR ARE WE?

As recently as 2001, the U.S. Central Command's public affairs system seems to have initially faired poorly during Operation Enduring Freedom in Afghanistan. In a December 2001 letter to the Pentagon Bureau Chiefs, Ms. Victoria Clark, Assistant Secretary of Defense for Public Affairs, apologized for "severe shortcomings in our [U.S. military] preparedness to support news organizations in their efforts to cover U.S. military operations in Afghanistan."

Sifting through a review of an After Action Review provided by one of the first military public affairs units in Afghanistan, the 49th Public Affairs Detachment from the 82nd Airborne Division, may shed some light into why Ms. Clark felt compelled to apologize for the military's shortcomings to support the media during the early stages of conflict. According to the AAR, submitted by U.S. Army Capt. Jimmie E. Cummings, Jr., the detachment's primary mission was to support the media and the secondary mission was to provide command information products.[66] Despite this being the first major ground operation since the Gulf War, the U.S. military may not have done its best to prepare this frontline public affairs unit for what would become one of the largest U.S. military news story since the Gulf War. Capt. Cummings states that the detachment essentially had five significant issues that negatively effected the execution of their mission. He lists the five issues as:

- Lack of a communications package.
- Divergent demands commanding and controlling of public affairs assets.
- Lack of detailed public affairs guidance at the frontlines.

16

- Institutional mistrust of media extended to Army journalists in executing missions with the 10th Mountain Division and with the U.S. Special Forces.
- Friction in strategic deploying into and redeploying out of theater.

Regarding the lack of a communications package, the detachment did not have the basic tools to communicate. Lack of dedicated phone lines, tactical FM radios, satellite phones, and even the placement of the detachment 90-minutes drive away from where the media were mostly located spelled trouble from the beginning. Not only could the detachment not get their command information products back in a timely manner, but the detachment also could not support the media. Very few of the media were willing to make the extremely dangerous 90-minute drive between Kabul, where most of the media centralized themselves to cover the conflict in Afghanistan, to the detachment's location at the Bagram Airbase. In addition, because the detachment lacked a dedicated phone line and telephone, the media did not have a military contact number to call when they needed information.

The detachment's third observation regarding the lack of public affairs guidance was probably tied to the second observation regarding the chains of command for public affairs. According to the detachment, there initially was no command or control over the public affairs operations during the critical first month of deployment (November-December 2001).[67] Later, the detachment was tasked organized under the Joint Special Operations Task Force, JSOTF-N. Then later, the detachment operated under the Combined Force Command Land Component Commander at Bagram. These multiple chains of command provided little public affairs guidance to the detachment and when they did, it contributed to confusing the public affairs personnel as the two chains of command often provided conflicting guidance.[68]

The detachment's fourth observation may be the most troublesome: institutional mistrust of media extended to Army journalists in the execution of their missions. This comment may be a two-edged sword in that it says something about a systemic mistrust by the U.S. military in Afghanistan toward journalists that spilled over to the U.S. public affairs personnel who were in essence "guilty by association." These ill feelings toward both journalists and military public affairs personnel did nothing to ease the American people's concern of their sons and daughters who were fighting under the harshest of conditions. Just how many stories of heroics or of unprecedented military capability may never be known because of this attitude of mistrust still engrained by some in today's military.

The fifth observation, I would say, is a criticism not unique to this public affairs detachment. There may not be one commander who does not wish that the higher headquarters staff did more to support their unit during a deployment, whether the deployment was to Afghanistan or to the National Training Center. Nevertheless, the point to take away from the detachment's frustration of having to do more than their fare share of coordinating for transportation and administration support is that losing commands need to ensure that every unit, large or small, deploys combat ready. The last thing a gaining commander may want in the heat of battle is to have a unit fall under their organization and be a sponge of critical resources that should have been provided at the unit's home station.

Nevertheless, public affairs support and operations appears to have improved in the following months. By the time the 28th Public Affairs Detachment from Fort Lewis, Washington, hit the ground in Bagram in June of 2002, it seems that many of the issues experienced by the 49th Public Affairs Detachment were solved. During a review of 28h Public Affairs Detachment's AAR, the unit's chain of command was the Combined Joint Task Force-180, under the command of Lieutenant General Dan McNeil of the 18th Airborne Corps. The 28th eventually built up its command information operation to produce a daily paper, six days a week. Unlike the primary mission of the 49th Public Affairs Detachment, the 28th's primary mission was command information. This is not to say that the detachment did not support the media, because they did, but it was not their primary mission.[69] What was not clear in the AAR, however, is if the change in focus away from the media was due to a continued institutional mistrust by the military.

WHY SHOULD THE MILITARY ENGAGE THE MEDIA ?

Why the military should engage the media is probably best stated by General (Ret) Dennis J. Reimer in a 1997 memorandum to his senior Army leaders. "Our success, as an institution, depends on the degree to which all senior leaders communicate clearly to the American people. It is in fact part of your METL [Mission Essential Task List]," said Reimer.[70]

In a recent personal discussion with the Commandant of the U.S. Army War College, Major General Robert R. Ivany said that public affairs has become essential to military operations and that he believed the military's senior leadership was onboard with engaging the media.[71] However, within 24 hours of that conversation a general who was at the War College for a presentation to the War College students said that he does not deal with the media. "You probably haven't seen my picture in the press in the last year and you won't. I let other officers deal with the media, because I don't."[72] This media avoidance attitude by a senior military leader says a lot about the current state of media relations...that we are not where we need to be.

Despite the attitude, current Department of Defense Directives places an overwhelming responsibility on Combatant Commanders to support the media via public affairs.[73] The following represents current DoD guidelines that require an extraordinary amount of planning as well as resourcing by the Combatant Commander:

- Journalists will be provided access to all major military units.
- Military public affairs personnel should act as liaisons, but should not interfere with the reporting process.
- Commanders should permit journalists to ride on military vehicles and aircraft, whenever feasible.
- Commanders will supply public affairs with facilities to enable timely, secure, compatible transmission of pool material.[74]

RECOMMENDATIONS

Having now looked at what scholars, journalists, and some in the military have said, combine those thoughts with a historical review of the military-media relationships, and three common trends become apparent as to why today there is still an unhealthy conflict between reporters and the military. The trends are: ad hoc organizations do not adequately respond to combatant commander needs or to the needs of the media, military public affairs personnel are not adequately resourced, and the military's aversion to engaging the media.

AD HOC ORGANIZATIONS:

One of the main problems is that the Combatant Commander's public affairs resources are stretched too thin to support the Sidle or Hoffman recommendations, while also supporting public affairs activities throughout the remaining area of operations to include those activities back at their home station. Joint Pub 3-61 also spells warning to commanders that their organization's public affairs office will be "inadequate to respond to the increase in news media and public interest" during crisis operations.[75]

For example, at the U.S. Southern Command, there are only four military public affairs officers at the headquarters to plan for and conduct public affairs activities in 32 countries of SOUTHCOM's area of responsibility.[76] During SOUTHCOM's humanitarian support to Central America in the aftermath of Hurricane Mitch in 1998, two of the four officers deployed out of the headquarters to Central America. Meanwhile, the two remaining officers, one of whom was the director of public affairs, were left with the responsibility to continue public affairs activities in the AOR, as well as continue community relations and command information activities.[77]

The SOUTHCOM deputy director for public affairs deployed to Honduras and eventually established Joint Information Bureaus in the Honduras, El Salvador, Guatemala, and Nicaragua. These Joint Information Bureaus were ad hoc organizations and were formed as public affairs units and individuals flowed into theater. For the most part, incoming public affairs personnel came from the Reserves and National Guard and rarely did they deploy as a unit. In essence, many of the Reserve units were pieced together with volunteers and would only stay in country for about two weeks. As great as the spirit of volunteerism is to the military, volunteers do not necessarily bring capability with them to do their mission. Only units bring with them transportation and communication systems, not individuals. Many Reserve public affairs units showed up in Central America without cameras, vehicles, communications systems, or even a government credit card. The two Joint Task Commanders, and two sub-JTF commanders, were often frustrated by not knowing what public affairs resources they would have from day-to-day, and with the continuous ebb and flow of public affairs personnel into and out of theater.[78]

Unlike engineer companies or artillery brigades, there is no standard JIB organization to provide support to Combatant Commanders. In essence, because there are no prescribed tables of organization for staffing or equipping a JIB, Combatant Commanders must piecemeal together the formation of a JIB from deploying public affairs personnel and units. Commanders can easily visualize the capabilities and logistic requirements of engineer, artillery, and armor units, but from what frame of reference do commanders use when told they will need to establish a JIB? There are no such DoD directives.

Therefore, a recommendation should be for a standing public affairs organization that would eliminate the current DoD ad hoc public affairs way of doing business. The Joint Force Command has taken the lead in this area and has experimented with a Joint Public Affairs Operations Groups (JPAOG) concept during its 2002 Millennium Challenge.[79] According to Lt. Col. Dave Lamp, public affairs officer at JFCOM, the JPAOG concept is designed to be a standing, rapid deployable, joint public affairs organization that can deploy within 48 hours of a Combatant Commander's request for public affairs support. Probably the best thought about the JPAOG is that it arrives fully resourced with equipment and personnel.

The JPAOG will not only provide support to the Combatant Commander's media operations, but it will also be the command and control of public affairs units and individuals from pre-deployment to the initial phases of an operation. The JPAOG will essentially be a fully resourced JIB augmenting the Combatant Commander for the first 60-90 days of an organization.[80] Once a sufficient numbers of public affairs personnel and units are in place to take over the JIB responsibilities, the JPAOG would redeploy back to JFCOM and prepare for the next operation.

This concept is certainly worth further study and analysis, but not at the cost of becoming lost in the bureaucracy of experimentation. In essence, DoD should fully resource this concept immediately and deploy it into the CENTCOM theater of operations in preparation for a possible U.S. invasion of Iraq. In this period of DoD transformation, DoD should move quickly to get this product on the street and then do product improvement down the road. This concept should greatly reduce a Combatant Commander's worry over media operations during the initial phases of battle because he will now have a fully functioning public affairs team from the first day of combat.

As noble an effort this is by JFCOM to test the JPAOG concept, the JPAOG only addresses the short-term needs of a commander. In essence, the JPAOG provides the Combatant Commander with a system that jump starts his public affairs effort and will redeploy back to JFCOM in 60-90 days. The last thing a Combatant Commander may want, however, is to have his public affairs command and controlling headquarters rotating out in the heat of battle after they have established relationships with his staff and the media. DoD should look at making taking this concept a more permanent part of the Combatant Commander's operations during conflict.

PUBLIC AFFAIRS NOT ADEQUATELY RESOURCED

Although the JPAOG will do a lot for setting the stage for success, it still does not address the fact that public affairs units and individuals deploy without sufficient resources to do their jobs. As mentioned previously with comments from LTC Perrich about the Gulf War and from Capt. Cummings in Afghanistan, commanders sometimes do poorly in providing adequate resources to their public affairs units.

This lack of resources, mainly with transportation and communication support, often translates to the media as a lack of preparedness by the military and may have long-term issues with the military's credibility. In essence, if the first contact the media have is with an unprepared and unresourced military public affairs officer, then the impression we leave with the media is that maybe the rest of the military operation is unprepared, too. If the military does not make a good first impression, its credibility certainly is at stake. As we know, it takes longer to establish credibility than to destroy one's credibility.

The recommendation here is that losing commanders should ensure that the public affairs personnel and units are well prepared and resourced to deploy. These personnel and units should not show up in a theater of operations as an immediate sponge of the Combatant Commander's assets. As with the media, if public affairs units show up unprepared their credibility is damaged with the Joint Task Force staff and as a result, may never receive the support they need.

Gaining commanders should also understand that unlike the arriving combat units into his AOR, public affairs units are doing their combat mission the day they arrive in theater. Therefore, it is essential that arriving public affairs units and personnel be provided not only logistical support, but are also are quickly accepted into the commander's staff. This can only happen if public affairs personnel are not treated, as Navy Captain Sherman said at the end of the Gulf War, "the bastard children of the operation."[81]

MILITARY'S AVERSION TO THE MEDIA

Whereas the first two trends are a matter of providing adequate resources to public affairs operations, the third trend may be more difficult to fix because it deals with the culture of the military. As we all know, culture is tough to change because it involves the hearts and minds of those in service. But, why after so many years since Vietnam is the military still reluctant to engage the media? Perhaps the military, although some senior leaders claim it is not so, is still in a zero-defect mentality where there is no reward for risk takers. After all, what are the gains to engaging the media when engaging the media can certainly have an immediate detrimental effect to one's career?

Many in the military still recall what happened in 1995 to Colonel Gregory Fontenot, the commander who led the first U.S. brigade into Bosnia, when he was quoted by an embedded reporter from the Wall Street Journal. Tom E. Ricks from the Journal quoted Fontenot of warning his African-American soldiers to be wary of what he described as racist Croats.[82] Fontenot also said that the U.S. would not be out of Bosnia in 12 months, which ran counter to what the Clinton Administration was saying at the time. Fontenot was castigated not only by the administration but also by the military for his comments. This, according to Charles C. Moskos, a military sociologist at MIT, had a "chilling effect on military personnel when journalists are around."[83]

A suggestion then, is that today's senior military leaders need to invest time and resources into transforming this media-adverse culture. It will take time, but so will the military's transformation into an Objective Force. The military cannot continue to have senior leaders setting the example by shying away from the media as their way of conducting public affairs. Because information is now global and what happens in the foxhole may now have strategic implications, it is important that we educate the masses to help in this cultural change in the military. All military schools should review their curriculums for instruction at preparing tomorrow's leaders for engaging the media. For example, during the first six months of this War College Class, there has been less than three hours of time directed to military-media relations. The War College does offer an elective for media-military relations, but it is not required. If this is truly the Information Age where the media can project real-time images of the battlefield, thus effecting strategic leaders emotions and decisions, then why is this last bastion of military schooling directing so little toward preparing tomorrow's senior leaders for the media?

CONCLUSION

Throughout American history, no matter the time or war, there has always been a conflict between the military and the media. Despite the Ernie Pyle's and at times, media savvy generals, the media's right to a free press conflicts with the military's concern for operational security. It serves no constructive purpose, however, to ignore this conflict nor does it serve a purpose by adding to it. Therefore, it is time for the U.S. military to accept the media as part of the battlefield of the 21st century, and to understand and prepare for the media as it does for other battlefield elements.

Few commanders, nor troops for that matter, like to conduct their operations in rain, snow, or when temperatures exceed 100 degrees. In today's press, many military analysts are saying that the attack into Iraq will take place no later than March of this year because the military does not want to fight in the heat of the summer months. Nevertheless, as much as commanders and troops may not like to fight in adverse weather, they plan and prepare for these battlefield conditions.

Commanders ensure that their troops receive not only the equipment, but also the training to survive in adverse battlefield environments. The point here is not to say that the media are equivalent to bad weather or pose an adverse environment, but to point out that no matter whether the military likes or dislikes the media, the media will be a part of the battlefield environment just as the weather. As is the case with inclement weather, the better the commander plans and prepares his or her troops, as well as themselves for the media, the better they and their troops will do when faced with a reporter.

As General Powel said in 1989 to his commanders prior to sending U.S. troops into Panama, "Once you've got all the forces moving and everything's being taken care of by the commander, turn your attention to television because you can win the battle or lose the war if you don't handle the story right."[84]

WORD COUNT=9,736

ENDNOTES

[1] John J. Fialka, <u>Hotel Warriors</u> (Baltimore: Johns Hopkins University Press, 1991), xi.

[2] Frank J. Stech, "Winning the CNN Wars." <u>Parameters</u>, U.S. Army War College (Autumn 1994): 12.

[3] General Ronald R. Fogleman, "Information Operations: The Fifth Dimension of Warfare," remarks delivered to the Armed Force Communications-Electronics Association, Washington, April 25, 1995.

[4] Maj. Gen. Charles W. McClain and Maj. Garry D. Levin, Public Affairs in America's 21st Century Army, <u>Military Review</u>, Vol. 74 Issue 11 (November 1994): 8; available from EBSCOhost; accessed 6 January 2001.

[5] McClain, 5.

[6] Pascale Combelles-Siegel. <u>The Troubled Path to Pentagon's Rules on Media Access to the Battlefield</u>. Strategy Research Project (Carlisle Barracks: U.S. Army War College, 15 May 1996), 4.

[7] Ibid., 8.

[8] Ibid., 34.

[9] Stephen P. Aubin, <u>Distorting Defense</u> (Westport, Connecticut: Praeger, 1998) 6.

[10] Ibid., 201.

[11] Lt. Col. Joseph G. Curtin, <u>Strategic Leaders: It's Time to Meet the Press</u>, Strategy Research Project (Carlisle Barracks: U.S. Army War College, 9 April 2002), iii.

[12] Ibid., 4.

[13] Ibid., 22.

[14] Loren B. Thompson, <u>Defense Beat</u> (New York: Lexington Books, 1991) 177.

[15] Fialka, 4-5.

[16] Debra Gersh, "Press restrictions must GO." <u>Editor & Publisher</u> (6 July 1991), 7.

[17] Ibid., 7.

[18] Steven Manning, "The Press vs. The Pentagon," <u>Scholastic Update</u> (22 Nov. 1991), 22.

[19] Fialka, 60.

[20] David Lamb, "Pentagon Hardball," <u>Washington Journalism Review</u> (April 1991), 34.

[21] Ibid., 34.

[22] Ibid., 34.

[23] Ibid., 35.

[24] Michael Emery and Edwin Emery, <u>The Press and America</u>, 4th ed. (New Jersey: Prentice Hall, 1978), 69.

[25] Ibid., 70.

[26] Ibid., 69.

[27] Thompson, 11.

[28] Johanna Neuman, <u>Lights, Camera, War</u> (New York: St Martin's Press, 1996), 26.

[29] Ibid., 33.

[30] Ibid., 33.

[31] Ibid., 34.

[32] Ibid., 39.

[33] "Reporting From the Front Lines – Timeline/WWI." Available from http://www.usnewsclassroom.com/resources/activities/war_reporting/timeline/ww1-censor.html; Internet; accessed 21 January 2003.

[34] "The First Amendment: 200th Anniversary," <u>Public Affairs Research Guide: Office, Chief of Public Affairs, Department of the Army</u>, (1991), 17.

[35] Neuman, 82.

[36] Curtin, 7.

[37] Neuman, 127.

[38] Daniels, 41.

[39] Dwight C. Daniels, <u>The Military and the Media: A Historical Perspective and Prospective Study of the Relationship</u>. Thesis Paper (University of Missouri-Colombia, 1985), 37.

[40] Joseph Mathews, <u>Reporting the Wars</u> (Minneapolis: The University of Minnesota Press, 1957), 177.

[41] John Steinbeck, <u>Once There Was A War</u> (New York: The Viking Press, 1958), p. xiii.

[42] Neuman, 43.

[43] Ibid., 49.

[44] Gannett Foundation Report, <u>The Media At War: The Press and the Persian Gulf Conflict</u> (New York: Gannett Foundation Media Center, 1991), 11.

[45] Daniels, 46.

[46] Neuman, 220

[47] The ideas in this paragraph are based on remarks made by several seminar students at the U.S. Army War College.

[48] John Friedman, "TV networks gird for war with Iraq," Jan. 1, 2003. And, Neil Hickey's article titled "The Pentagon's War Reporting Rules are the Toughest Ever," February 2002; available from CBS.MarketWatch; accessed 2 January 2003.

[49] William H. Hammond, "The Army Public Affairs: Enduring Principles," <u>Parameters</u> (June 1989), 69.

[50] Ibid., 70.

[51] Richard L. Upchurch, "Wanted: A Fair Press," <u>Proceedings</u> (July 1984), 68.

[52] Neuman, 175.

[53] Joseph Metcalf, "The Mother of the Mother," <u>Proceedings</u> (April 1986), 56.

[54] Combelles-Siegel, 5.

[55] Ibid., 7.

[56] Peter Young, <u>The Media and the Military</u> (New York: St. Martin's Press, 1997), 147.

[57] ibid., 17

[58] <u>Facts on File</u>, "Persian Gulf Press Rules Issued." Jan. 10, 1991 4-5.

[59] Ibid., 14.

[60] Ibid., 15.

[61] Walter Cronkite, "What is There to Hide?" <u>Newsweek,</u> 25 February 1991, 43.

[62] David Gergen, "Why America Hates The Press," <u>U.S. News & World Report</u>, 11 March 1991, 57.

[63] Fialka, 5.

[64] Combelles-Siegel cites Major Kenneth S. Plato, USMC, <u>Military-Media Relations: First Impressions of Operations Desert Shield</u>, Individual Study Project (Newport, RI: Naval War College, February 11, 1995), 12.

[65] Perrich, 2.

[66] Capt. Jimmie E. Cummings and SFC Christopher J. Fletcher, 49th Public Affairs Detachment, 82nd Airborne Division After Action Review – Report/Lessons Learned Operation Enduring Freedom, 18 October 2001 – 8 February 2002, p. 1. This AAR was provided by the Army Public Affairs Center via e-mail in December 2002.

[67] Ibid., 4.

[68] Ibid., 4.

[69] Capt. Timothy M. Beninato and SSG Rhonda M. Lawson, 28th Public Affairs Detachment, CJTF-180, Bagram, Afghanistan, After Action Report/Lessons Learned, 3 June 2002 – 13 December 2002, p. 1. This AAR was provided by the Army Public Affairs Center via e-mail in December 2002.

[70] General Dennis J. Reimer, "Army-Media Relations," memorandum for Army leaders, Washington, D.C., 26 September 1997.

[71] During a discussion with MG Ivany about information operations and public affairs, it was his opinion that senior military leaders were open and willing to engage the media. In essence, that times had changed since Vietnam and leaders were engaging the press.

[72] Personal recollection from Course II of the Army War College, 2002.

[73] Joint Pub 3-61, <u>Doctrine for Public Affairs in Joint Operations</u> (Washington, D.C.: 14 May 1997), II-1.

[74] Ibid., III2-4.

[75] Ibid., ix.

[76] The author served in SOUTHCOM from 1998 to 2000 as the deputy director for public affairs. During that period, he deployed to Central America, establishing Joint Information Bureaus in the Honduras, Guatemala, El Salvador, and Nicaragua in support of Hurricane Mitch disaster relief.

[77] Ibid., personal recollections.

[78] Ibid., personal recollections.

[79] JO2 Anthony Falvo, "Joint Concept Puts Public Affairs Professionals on the Media Battlefield," 7 August, 2002. Lt. Col. Dave Lamp, a public affairs officer at the Joint Force Command has been very helpful in providing information regarding the JPAOG. Although this article was sent to the author by Lt. Col. Lamp, it can be accessed on the Joint Forces Command Home Page.

[80] Lt. Col. Dave Lamp, provided a concept brochure on the Joint Public Affairs Operations Group, 12 December 2002.

[81] Combelles-Siegel, 16.

[82] Charles C. Moskos, The Media and the Military in Peace and Humanitarian Operations (Chicago: McCormick Tribune Foundation, 2000), 26.

[83] Ibid., 26.

[84] Bob Woodward, The Commanders (New York: Simon and Schuster, 1991), 155.

BIBLIOGRAPHY

Aubin, Stephen P. Distorting Defense. Westport, Connecticut: Praeger, 1998.

Beninato, Timothy M. Capt. And Lawson, Rhonda M. SSG. 28th Public Affairs Detachment, CJTF-180, Bagram, Afghanistan After Action Report/Lessons Learned 3 June 2002 to 13 December 2002.

Clark, Victoria, ASD for Public Affairs. "Media Coverage Issues." Memorandum for News Bureau Chiefs. Washington, D.C., 6 December 2001.

Clark, Victoria, ASD for Public Affairs. Minutes of a Meeting with DoD National Media Pool Bureau Chiefs, Washington, The Pentagon, 13 December 2001.

Combelles-Siegel, Pascale. The Troubled Path to the Pentagon's Rules on Media Access to the Battlefield: Grenada to Today. MacArthur Foundation Study. Carlisle Barracks: U.S. Army War College, 15 May 1996.

"Conduct of the Persian Gulf War, Final Report to Congress," Washington: Government Printing Office, April 1992.

Cronkite, Walter. "What is There to Hide?" Newsweek, 25 February 1991, 43.

Cummings, Jimmie E. Capt. And Fletcher, Christopher J. SFC. 49th Public Affairs Detachment After Action Review – Report/Lessons Learned Operation Enduring Freedom 18 October 2001 to 8 February 2002.

Curtin, Joseph G. LTC. Strategic Leaders: It's Time to Meet the Press. Strategy Research Project. Carlisle Barracks: U.S. Army War College, 9 April 2002.

Daniels, Dwight C. The Military and the Media: A Historical Perspective and Prospective Study of the Relationship. Thesis Paper. University of Missouri-Colombia, 1985.

Emery, Edwin, and Michael Emery. The Press and America 4th ed. New Jersey: Prentice Hall, 1978.

Falvo, Anthony JO2. "Joint Concept Puts Public Affairs Professionals on the Media Battlefield" Article was provided via e-mail by Lt. Col. Dave Lamp from the Joint Forces Command <lampdh@JFCOM.mil>. Internet.

Fialka, John. Hotel Warriors: Covering the Gulf War. Baltimore: The John Hopkins University Press, 1991.

Fogleman, Ronald R. Gen. "Information Operations: The Fifth Dimension of Warfare," remarks delivered to the Armed Force Communications-Electronics Association, Washington, D.C., 25 April 1995.

Friedman, John. TV networks gird for war with Iraq. January 2003. Available from <CBS.MarketWatch.com>. Accessed 2 January 2003.

Gannett Foundation Report. <u>The Media At War: The Press and the Persian Gulf Conflict</u>. New York: Gannett Foundation Media Center, 1991.

Gergen, David. "Why America Hates the Press," <u>U.S. News & World Report</u>, (11 March 1991): 57.

Gersh, Debra. "Press Restrictions Must Go." <u>Editor & Publisher</u>, (6 July 1991): 7-8.

Hammond, William H. "The Army Public Affairs: Enduring Principles." <u>Parameters</u> (June 1989): 69.

Hickey, Neil. <u>The Pentagon's War Reporting Rules are the Toughest Ever</u>. February 2002. Available from <CBS.MarketWatch.com>. Accessed 2 January 2003.

Joint Pub 3-61. <u>Doctrine for Public Affairs in Joint Operations</u>. Washington, D.C.: 14 May 1997.

Lamb, David. "Pentagon Hardball." <u>Washington Journal Review</u> (April 1991): 34.

Manning, Steven. "The Press vs. The Pentagon." <u>Scholastic Update</u> (22 November 1991): 22.

Matthews, Joseph. <u>Reporting the Wars</u>. Minneapolis: The University of Minnesota Press, 1957.

McClain, Charles W. Maj. Gen. and Levin, Garry D. Maj., "Public Affairs in the 21st Century Army," <u>Military Review</u> 74 (November 1994): 8.

Metcalf, Joseph. "The Mother of the Mother." <u>Proceedings</u> (April 1986): 52-56.

Moskos, Charles C. <u>The Media and the Military in Peace and Humanitarian Operations</u>. Chicago: McCormick Tribune Foundation (2000): 26.

Neuman, Johanna. <u>Lights, Camera, War</u>. New York: St. Martin's Press, 1996.

Northup, Zac. "The Wrong Media for the Right War." <u>National Guard Review</u> (Summer 2002): 8-10.

Perrich, Robert A., Lt. Col., Letter to Pete Williams, ASD for Public Affairs, regarding his thoughts on John Fialka's Book "Hotel Warriors." Fort Carson, Colorado, 17 June 1992.

"Persian Gulf Press Rules Issued." <u>Facts on File</u> (10 January 1991): 4-5.

Reimer, Dennis J. Gen. "Army-Media Relations." Memorandum for Army Leaders. Washington, D.C., 26 September 1997.

"Reporting From the Front Lines – Timeline/WWI." Available from http://www.usnewsclassroom.com/resources/activities/war_reporting/time__line/ww1-censor.html. Accessed 21 January 2003.

Schmeisser, Peter. "Shooting Pool." <u>The New Republic</u> (March 18,1991): 22.

Stech, Frank J. "Winning the CNN Wars," <u>Parameters</u> (Autumn 1994): 12.

Steinbeck, John. <u>Once There Was a War</u>. New York: The Viking Press, 1958.

Tebbel, John. <u>The Media in America</u> Thomas Y. Crowell Company, 1974.

Thompson, Loren B. <u>Defense Beat</u>. New York: Lexington Books, 1991.

"The First Amendment: 200th Anniversary." <u>Public Affairs Research Guide: Office, Chief of Public Affairs</u>, Department of the Army, 1991.

United States Information Agency. "The Media and Their Messages." Available from <http://usinfo.state.gov/usa/infousa/facts/factover/ch12.htm>; Internet: accessed 21 September 2002.

Upchurch, Richard L. "Wanted: A Fair Press." <u>Proceedings</u> (July 1984): 68.

Woodward, Bob. <u>The Commanders</u>. New York: Simon and Schuster, 1991.

Young, Peter. <u>The Media and the Military</u>. New York: St. Martin's Press, 1997.

www.ingramcontent.com/pod-product-compliance
Lightning Source LLC
Chambersburg PA
CBHW052025280526
45793CB00005B/1121